# Up the Hill

by Tamera Williams
illustrated by Tammie Lyon

Practice Decodable 4

Mc Graw Hill Education

Bothell, WA • Chicago, IL • Columbus, OH • New York, NY

**MHEonline.com**



Send all inquiries to:
McGraw-Hill Education
8787 Orion Place
Columbus, OH 43240

ISBN: 978-0-02-145970-4
MHID: 0-02-145970-3

Printed in China

8 9 10 11 12 DSS 27 26 25 24 23

There is a .
hill

There is a  up the .

school hill

There is a  .

bus

The 

is up.

The  is up.

bus

There is a  !

school